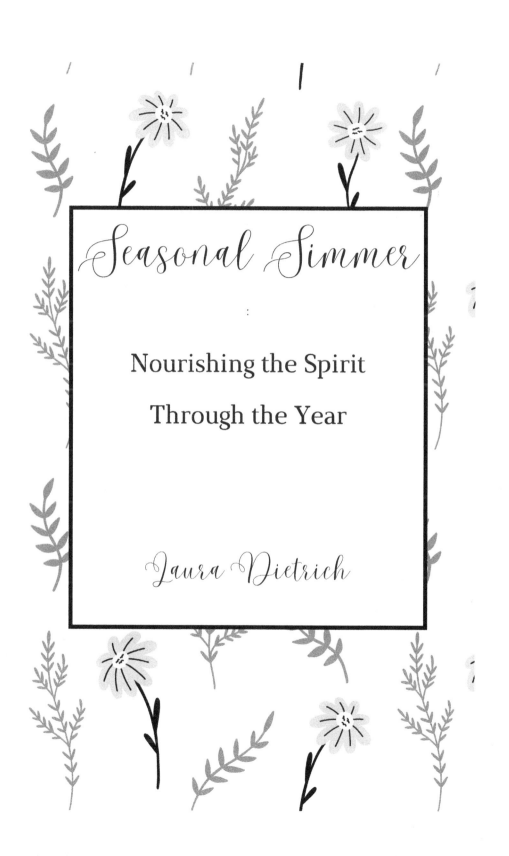

Seasonal Simmer

Nourishing the Spirit

Through the Year

Laura Dietrich

A Dedication

In the heart of our kitchen, where laughter and stories merge with the fragrant melodies of simmering pots, this book finds its truest inspiration. To my dear Grandma, whose timeless wisdom and culinary magic filled our home with warmth; to Aunt Jeanie, whose skillful hands and endless creativity turned ingredients into art; to Mema, whose recipes whispered of generations past and love's enduring embrace; and to my cherished Mom, whose guidance and love have shaped every dish and every memory.

Table of Contents

Introduction

Nourishing the Spirit Through Scent

In a world brimming with constant motion and digital chaos, there exists a timeless, soothing connection to be rekindled—the ancient art of simmering. Beyond the bubbling pots of soups and stews lies a realm of enchantment that transcends the kitchen, reaching into the very essence of our souls.

Welcome to "Seasonal Simmer: Nourishing the Spirit Through the Year," a book that invites you on a journey through the seasons, guided by the aromatic alchemy of spiritual simmer pots. Together we will introduce your senses and your home to the practice of using different ingredients to bring about a positive intention filled experience.

Our sense of smell serves as a powerful bridge to our memories, evoking vivid recollections of both our past experiences and the present moments we cherish. Recall the comforting scent of freshly baked cookies at your grandmother's house? How the aroma of cinnamon instantly transports us to the heartwarming Holiday Season.

When we engage in the thoughtful process of selecting ingredients and mindfully crafting a simmer pot, we not only infuse our homes with delightful fragrances but also establish a meaningful connection to timeless traditions while forging new memories.

This act becomes a poignant reminder of the old ways and the beautiful opportunity to create fresh associations that will be treasured for years to come.

As the Earth dances through its annual cycle, each turn of the wheel presents an opportunity to attune ourselves with nature's rhythm. The seasons offer us gifts, from the vibrant bloom of spring to the quiet introspection of winter. Within these pages, you will find a collection of monthly recipes that align with the ever-changing energies of the natural world, weaving together flavors, scents, and intentions.

Imagine stepping into your kitchen, where a symphony of ingredients awaits—a melody of herbs, fruits, spices, and dreams. Each recipe is a carefully crafted blend, not only of edible delights but also of intention and mindfulness.

The Wheel of the Year

In the circle of seasons, the wheel does turn,
A rhythmic dance of nature, as we discern,
The cycle of life, the changing of the year,
In every phase, a lesson to revere.

At winter's solemn edge, the wheel begins,
As nature rests, and frosty silence wins.
In stillness, we reflect, in hearth's warm glow,
Finding wisdom in the quiet, in the snow.

With the onset of spring, the wheel takes flight,
As life awakens, colors burst forth bright.
Blossoms bloom, and creatures stir with glee,
In rebirth's tender embrace, we are set free.

Summer, oh, summer, in the wheel's grand spin,
The world alive with warmth, the days stretch thin.
Fields sway with golden grains, the sun shines high,
In abundance and in joy, we touch the sky.

Then autumn's golden touch, a bittersweet grace,
As leaves cascade like memories in the chase.
Harvest's bounty gathered, the earth provides,
A season of reflection as daylight slides.

In the wheel of the year, we find our place,
A reminder of life's ever-changing grace.
Each turn of the wheel, a chapter to explore,
In nature's timeless cycle, we seek more.

With every season's shift, a chance to grow,
To learn, to love, to change, to let go.
In the circle of seasons, our lives entwine,
As the wheel of the year, forever divine.

A History

Simmering Through Time

The history of using simmer pots with intentions is deeply intertwined with ancient practices of aromatics, herbalism, and spiritual rituals. This art has evolved across cultures and centuries, serving as a bridge between the material and spiritual worlds. While the specific origins are challenging to trace, the use of simmer pots for both practical and metaphysical purposes can be found throughout human history.

Ancient Traditions

In ancient civilizations such as Egypt, Greece, and Rome, the use of aromatic herbs and spices was common for both religious and medicinal purposes. These cultures recognized the power of fragrances to enhance spiritual connections, purify spaces, and promote well-being. The fragrant smoke of resins like frankincense and myrrh was often used as offerings to deities and spirits, setting the stage for the later development of simmer pot practices. Herbs have held a significant place in human history, not only as sources of sustenance and medicine but also as symbols of spirituality and connection.

The Bible, one of the world's most ancient texts, contains references to various herbs that were valued for their diverse uses. Throughout history, numerous herbs have been employed to combat and prevent diseases, illnesses, and infections, spanning millennia. Many of these very herbs are interwoven within the biblical narratives. From alleviating sore throats to combating depression, you might be amazed by the array of healing herbs from the Bible that possess the potential to enhance your holistic well-being. Among these are aloes, cumin, cinnamon, cassia, hyssop, garlic, mustard, mint, frankincense, myrrh, saffron, and anise.

Mediaeval Herbalism and Alchemy

During the medieval period, herbalism and alchemy played significant roles in the development of simmer pot traditions. Monks and scholars cultivated gardens of healing herbs, using them to create elixirs, tinctures, and fragrances. These concoctions were believed to possess both physical and metaphysical properties. Alchemical practices focused on the transformation of substances, which extended to the idea that fragrant blends could transform the energies of a space or individual.

The use of herbs held a central place in daily life for those living in the medieval time period, influencing everything from medicine and cuisine to spirituality and folklore. People of the Middle Ages relied on herbs for various purposes, and their knowledge of these botanical treasures was often passed down through generations.

Herbs were used to create fragrances and perfumes in the form of sachets, pomanders, and scented oils. These fragrant preparations were used to mask unpleasant odors and were believed to have protective and healing properties. Lavender, rose petals, and rosemary were commonly used in these aromatic concoctions. Herbs also held spiritual significance and were believed to possess mystical and protective qualities. They were used in religious rituals, often burned as incense or used in simmer pots. Herbs like sage and frankincense were associated with purification and were used to cleanse spaces and individuals spiritually.

Folk Traditions

As societies shifted into the Renaissance and beyond, the practice of using simmer pots took on a more domestic and folkloric role. Ingredients from the kitchen and garden were combined with intention to create magical brews. Simmer pots were used not only for scent but also as tools for manifestation, protection, and connecting with the spirit realm. Simmer pots have a history that reaches far back to an era when the hearth reigned as the heart of the home—a time when humanity existed in close harmony with the earth, sky, and the elemental forces. In those days, plants, herbs, and spices held significance not only as sustenance but as remedies for body, mind , and soul.

Positioned atop the hearth, the simmer pot would gradually heat up throughout the day, releasing the cherished essence of the natural world that surrounded you. Its aroma, shifting with the rhythm of the seasons, would infuse your dwelling with the sacred tapestry of your environment. These practices were often passed down through generations, with each family adding their unique twists.

Modern Resurgance

In recent years, there has been a resurgence of interest in holistic well-being, mindfulness, and spiritual practices. Simmer pots have found their place within this movement, offering a blend of ancient wisdom and contemporary intention-setting. People seek ways to create sacred spaces, enhance mindfulness, and align their energies with the natural world. Simmer pots provide a tangible and sensory experience, combining the power of intention with the comforting rituals of the kitchen. There has also been an interest in chemical free options to make your home smell amazing. Being able to use elements of your choosing allows a total customization of the scent and the intentions. It is also perfect for those who are sensitive to candle smoke or incense. With the rise of aromatherapy and the understanding of how scents affect mood and emotions, simmer pots have gained recognition as tools for intentional aromatherapy. The careful selection and combination of ingredients offer a multi-layered experience—aroma, symbolism, and intention—that can influence a person's mental, emotional, and spiritual state.

Today and Beyond

In the modern world, simmer pots with intentions are embraced by those seeking to infuse their daily lives with purpose and mindfulness. The practice transcends cultural boundaries, allowing individuals to personalize their creations based on their beliefs and experiences. Whether used for religious connections, meditation, or simply creating a soothing atmosphere, simmer pots continue to connect people with ancient traditions while adapting to the needs of contemporary spiritual seekers.

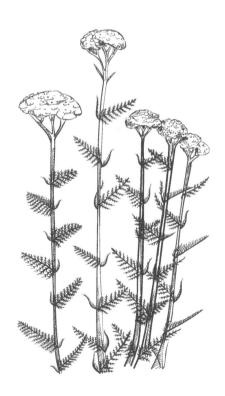

Seasonal Simmer

In a kitchen bathed in candlelight's soft glow,
An herbal simmer pot with intentions starts to grow.
Each herb and spice, a whisper from the earth's
embrace,
With purpose and with meaning, in this sacred space.

Lavender, with calming grace, takes center stage,
To soothe our weary souls, and minds engage.
Rosemary, a guardian of memory and might,
Invites clarity of thought, and dreams to take flight.

Mint, with its refreshing zing, is there to mend,
To heal the spirit, and wounds to tend.
Sage, the sage of wisdom, lends its sage advice,
Guiding us toward truth and virtue, oh so nice.

Basil brings its love and passion to the brew,
A heartfelt potion, for connection that is true.
Cinnamon, with warmth and spice, ignites desire,
A simmering love potion, a burning fire.

With a whisper of intention, hearts align,
In this herbal cauldron, where energies entwine.
For healing, love, or wisdom, whatever be the aim,
The simmer pot's intentions, it will gently claim.

As it bubbles on the stove, and fragrances ascend,
Our dreams and hopes in this concoction blend.
With every simmered moment, spirits soar,
As we manifest our intentions more and more.

So, in the kitchen's sacred light, we brew and stew,
Our herbal simmer pot, intentions tried and true.
A potion of the heart, a potion of the soul,
In its mystical alchemy, we find our goal.

Elements

Finding Your Simmer Pot Elements

Gathering the elements you wish to incorporate into your simmer pot can be as simple as a visit to your local farmer's market or a leisurely stroll around your neighborhood. Gathering and collecting your ingredients can be a fulfilling part of your simmer pot experience. Taking time to forage and gather not only enhances your recipe but gives you the opportunity to bring a bit of the outdoors into your home. This is also the perfect opportunity to use fruits and herbs that have out lived their chance to be consumed. There is no need to toss these ingredients. You are simply giving them a new purpose.

Some of my favorite places to find elements:
- Your fridge or pantry
- Farmer's Market
- Bulk herb Shop
- Grow your own
- Forage in nature
- Online sources like Amazon and Etsy
- Natural Food Store
- Essential Oils

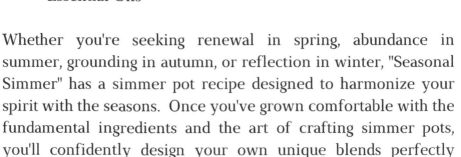

Whether you're seeking renewal in spring, abundance in summer, grounding in autumn, or reflection in winter, "Seasonal Simmer" has a simmer pot recipe designed to harmonize your spirit with the seasons. Once you've grown comfortable with the fundamental ingredients and the art of crafting simmer pots, you'll confidently design your own unique blends perfectly tailored for your household and loved ones.

Elements and Their Intentions

Beyond the tangible ingredients lies the heart of these recipes—ritual, thought, and intention. Just as our ancestors gathered around hearths and shared stories, we can cultivate sacred moments by kindling the flame beneath a simmer pot. The aromatic tendrils that rise from the pot carry our intentions to the universe, creating a connection that transcends time and space. The simmer pot's aroma will tangibly evoke the intentions you imbued while crafting your ingredients.

Common Elements

Allspice (Pimenta dioica)

Meaning and Intention: compassion, love, and luck
Folklore and Facts: Allspice was named so because the taste of it's berry is like a combination of clove, cinnamon, and nutmeg. It originated in Jamaica.

Anise (Pimpinella anisum)

Meaning and Intention: protection, purification, clarity, boldness , excitement, and restoration
Folklore and Facts: Anise under your pillow is said to keep away bad dreams. Its star-shape form is said to symbolize the connection between the earthly and celestial realms.

Ash (Fraxinus excelsior)
Meaning and Intention: greatness, growth, perspective
Folklore and Facts: In the Ancient Greek tradition the clouds were perceived as the expansive canopy of a legendary Ash tree, an entity considered the father of the world.

Balsam Fir (Abies balsamea)
Meaning and Intention: friendship, remembrance, honesty, progress, resilience
Folklore and Facts: The needles of the Balsam Fir are sharp and the oil smells like the quintessential Christmas tree.

Basil (Ocimum basilicum)
Meaning and Intention: romance, luck, good wishes
Folklore and Facts: In Italy, basil holds the emblematic role of representing love and is often employed as a gesture of affection.

Bay Laurel (Laurus nobilis)
Meaning and Intention: success, wishes, protections, manifestation, fame, love, achievement
Folklore and Facts: The Ancient Greeks crowned their best athletes, poets, and leaders, with a wreath made of Bay Laurel leaves. Bay was also used as a token of protection to those going off to battle.

Bittersweet (Celastrus scandens)
Meaning and Intention: honesty and truth
Folklore and Facts: The bittersweet blooms a beautiful cluster of bright orange blossoms. In the past it was worn in a pouch to protect the wearer from evil.

Black Pepper (Piper nigrum)
Meaning and Intention: fidelity, energy, love, protection
Folklore and Facts: At one point, Black Pepper was considered to be so important that it was used at a form of currency. It was usually only found in the homes of the aristocracy.

Black Tea (Camellia sinensis)
Meaning and Intention: constancy, contentment spiritual awakening, peace, courage, and connection
Folklore and Facts: A cup of Black Tea is said to be a remedy for a variety of ailments including fatigue, poor spirits, lightheadedness, and headaches.

Black Walnut (Juglans nigra)
Meaning and Intention: fertility, intellect, strategy, energy, health
Folklore and Facts: Black Walnut can be used to produce a natural brown dye. Over the years, Black Walnuts have often been a symbol of wisdom and discernment,

Buckthorn (Rhamnus cathartica)

Meaning and Intention: energy, enchantment, luck, and protection

Folklore and Facts: Buckthorn berries can be used to produce a vegetable dye that ranges from soft rust to pink.

Caraway (Carum carvi)

Meaning and Intention: faithfulness, health, love, and learning, passion, and wisdom

Folklore and Facts: Caraway seeds were a popular ingredient in love potions during the Middle Ages. It was thought to insure a lover from having wandering eyes.

Cardamom (Elettaria cardamomum

Meaning and Intention: Peaceful thoughts, love, and energy

Folklore and Facts: Cardamom has been in use since the 4th century. It is the 3rd most expensive spice in the world and is sometimes referred to as the "Queen of Spice".

Cinnamon (Cinnamomum verum)

Meaning and Intention: forgiveness, prosperity abundance, protection, and spirituality.

Folklore and Facts: The ancient Egyptians used cinnamon in their recipe for kyphi, an aromatic used for burning as well as in the practice of mummification.

Clove (Syzygium aromaticum)

Meaning and Intention: protection, purification, love, courage, peace and friendship

Folklore and Facts: For an easy home-made disinfectant, simply mix Clove oil and water in a spray bottle. It is said that Clove as am aromatic will get rid of negative energy, bring peace, and attract the opposite sex.

Coffee (Coffee arabica)

Meaning and Intention: camaraderie, friendship, loyalty, and happiness, and joy

Folklore and Facts: Coffee beans are often used to clear scent from the nose.

Cranberry (Vaccinium oxycoccus)

Meaning and Intentions: abundance, partnership, unity, gratitude, healing, and rejuvenation

Folklore and Facts: Cranberries are often used as a symbol during harvest festivals like Halloween (Samhain) and Christmas (Yule). Native Americans often used cranberries to make dye for textiles.

Cypress (Cupressus sempervirens)

Meaning and Intention: help through death and sorrow health

Folklore and Facts: Planting a Cypress tree on your property is said to bring you protection and blessings. During times of extreme sadness and mourning, using Cypress as an aromatic can bring you emotional strength.

Chamomile (Chamaemelum nobile)

Meaning and Intention: patience, love, sleep, wisdom, wealth, energy, initiative

Folklore and Facts: If planted near other weak plants, Chamomile is said to strengthen them. A soothing warm cup of Chamomile tea can soothe restlessness and encourage sleep.

Dill (Anethum graveolens)

Meaning and Intention: cheer, luck, and happiness

Folklore and Facts: In the Norse tradition, babies were given Dill seeds to help them sleep. Bundles of dill were hung on a baby cradle for protection.

Eucalyptus-Tasmanian Blue Gum (Eucalyptus globus)

Meaning and Intention: growth, healing, purification

Folklore and Fact: When used as an aromatic, Eucalyptus can be used to reduce stress and anxiety. In the folklore tradition of the Aboriginal people of Australia, the Eucalyptus is said to represent the separation of Earth from Heaven.

Frankincense (Boswellia sacra)

Meaning and Intention: sanctity, meditation, purification, protection, spirituality

Folklore and Facts: Frankincense is well known for being one of the three gifts brought to the newborn Jesus of Nazareth by the Three Magi. It has a long history as being used it religious rituals as it was believed that the smoke and aroma could carry prayers and petitions upward to heaven.

Ginger (Zingiber officinale)

Meaning and Intention: safety, strength, comfort, stability

Folklore and Facts: Ginger worn in a pouch was said to bring good luck to the wearer. Ginger has been used to ease digestive issues for hundreds of years.

Heather (Calluna vulgaris)

Meaning and Intention: beauty, good luck, inner healing, protection, purity, romance

Folklore and Facts: In the past, brooms were made by gathering twigs of Heather. Not only did it help to clean but was thought to offer protection to the household.

Juniper (Juniperus communis)

Meaning and Intention: cleanse, bless, protection, healing banishing negativity, purification

Folklore and Facts: Juniper berries can be used to flavor Gin or other alcohol. Olympians were given Juniper berries by the Ancient Greeks because it was thought to give them stamina during competition.

Lavender (Lavandula angustifolia)

Meaning and Intention: constancy, devotion, faith, love, humility, trust

Folklore and Facts: Lavender as an aromatic has been used to bring peacefulness to a home since ancient times. It has also been used to freshen linens and the body.

Lemon (Citrus limon)

Meaning and Intentions: patience, pleasant thoughts, gratitude, promises kept, protection, friendship, purification

Folklore and Facts: As an aromatic, lemon is often used to uplift the spirit and refresh your mood

Marjoram (Origanum majorana)

Meaning and Intentions: comfort, consolation, love, joy, health, and happiness

Folklore and Facts: Ancient people believed that Marjoram found growing on a grave indicated that the deceased was happy in the after life.

Nutmeg (Myristica fragrans)

Meaning and Intentions: clarity, love, health, protection, spirituality, and luck

Folklore and Facts: Nutmeg was once so valuable that nations went to war to control it.

Orange (Citrus sinensis)

Meaning and Intentions: meditation, compassion, simplicity, happiness, hope, new beginnings, and abundance

Folklore and Facts: Seen as symbols of purity and eternal love, oranges were often used in garlands, bouquets and adornments for brides in Victorian times.

Oregano (Origanum vulgare)

Meaning and Intentions: good luck, joy, happiness, soothing the soul, prophetic dreams
Folklore and Facts: According to the Ancient Greeks, Aphrodite herself created Oregano and planted it in her own garden.

Patchouli (Pogostemon cablin)

Meaning and Intention: abundance, help through conflict and anger, healing, and friendship
Folklore and Facts: Nervousness, tension, and worry can simply melt away when Patchouli is used as an aromatic.

Peppermint (Mentha piperita)

Meaning and Intention: love, rejuvenation, healing, cleansing
Folklore and Facts: The scent of Peppermint is so effective you can simply sniff it's leaves to assist with restlessness and sleep.

Pine (Pinus pinus)

Meaning and Intention: wisdom, longevity, protection, steadiness, and courage
Folklore and Facts: In many cultures, the Pine Tree was seen as a symbol of peace and long life. That is why "tree hugging" became popular. It was said that giving a pine a hug would give you a long life.

Rose (Rosa rubiginosa)

Meaning and Intention: adoration, love, beauty, passion, romance, elegance, luxury, and rebirth

Folklore and Facts: The Nez Perce and Salish believed that having roses around would protect them from evil spirits.

Rosemary (Salvia rosmarinus)

Meaning and Intention: remembrance, clarity, friendship, love, focus, and loyalty

Folklore and Facts: Rosemary under your pillow is said to keep away nightmares. If you smell Rosemary on Christmas Eve it is said that you will be happy throughout the coming year.

Sage (Salvia officinalis)

Meaning and Intention: holiness, long life, wisdom, respect, honor, cleansing, and artistic abilities

Folklore and Facts: In the Ancient Roman tradition Sage was said to be powerful enough to make someone immortal. In the Middle Ages, Sage was scattered on the floor to release it's aroma when stepped on.

Sandalwood (Santalum album)

Meaning and Intention: cleverness, meditation, faith, energy, memory, protection, travel safety, and creativity

Folklore and Facts: Sandalwood is able to hold its scent within it's wood for decades and is one of the most expensive types of wood because it is a threatened species.

Spearmint (Mentha spicata)

Meaning and Intention: love, warm feelings, sentimental feelings, virtue, mental clarity

Folklore and Facts: When used as an aromatic, Spearmint can help ease tension, help with focus, and allows concentration.

Sugar Maple (Acer saccharum)

Meaning and Intention: energy, longevity, love, and financial stability

Folklore and Facts: The paired seed of the Sugar Maple go by many names including helicopters, maple keys, and whirlybirds. Some Sugar Maples have been known to live up to 300 years.

Tarragon (Artemisia dracunculus)

Meaning and Intention: lasting commitment, permanence, protection

Folklore and Facts: Tarragon is one of four primary herbs in French cooking. Chewing Tarragon was a way the Ancient Greeks were able to relieve tooth pain.

Tea Tree (Melaleuca alternifolia)

Meaning and Intentions: communication, and healing

Folklore and Facts: Tea Tree oil has been shown to have both antibacterial and antiseptic properties. It can be used to treat acne, dandruff, and even lice.

Thyme (Thymus vulgaris)

Meaning and Intention: affection, bravery, courage, love, strength, restful sleep, happiness, healing, and energy

Folklore and Facts: A sprig of Thyme was a common embellishment on the scarves of knights on their way to fight in the Crusades. This was typically embroidered by the knight's lady.

Vanilla (Vanilla planifolia)

Meaning and Intention: comfort, welcoming, warm, love, good luck, and love

Folklore and Facts: In it's native habitat in Mexico, the Vanilla vine can grow up to 75 feet tall. The vanilla flavor we have come to know comes from the seed pods.

Witch Hazel (Hamamelis virginiana)

Meaning and Intention: protection, divination, and energy

Folklore and Facts: Witch Hazel is considered to be the most effective wood to use as a divining rod. This practice may have started in Germany in the fifteenth century. Witch Hazel was used by the Iroquois for it's antiseptic and astringent properties. It was often used to reduce swelling and prevent infection.

Yarrow (Achillea millefolium)

Meaning and Intention: courage, recovery, lasting love, protection, healing, and joy

Folklore and Facts: In the Middle Ages, Yarrow was used to repel lice, ticks, moths, and fleas. Some believe that Yarrow was the first herb given to baby Jesus and so became a token of luck.

Remember that the power of a simmer pot lies not only in the individual ingredients but in the intention you infuse them with. When creating your simmer pot, take a moment to set your intentions clearly, focusing on the energy you wish to bring into your space and life. As the pot simmers, visualize your desires coming to fruition and allow the aromatic steam to carry your intentions out into the universe.

Embracing the practice of incorporating simmer pots into your life can be a profound and transformative experience, leading to a multitude of positive effects that ripple through your days and beyond. These simple, yet intentional, rituals have the power to touch upon various aspects of your well-being, from your physical space to your emotional state, and from your spiritual connection to your daily mindset.

Instructions for your simmer pot

- Fill a pot with water, about halfway full.
- Add the ingredients listed for the specific month's simmer pot.
- Place the pot on the stove and bring the water to a gentle simmer.
- Lower the heat and allow the ingredients to infuse the water with their scents and energies.
- Keep an eye on the water level and add more if needed to prevent it from drying out.
- As the simmer pot releases its aromatic steam, take a moment to set your intentions for the month, visualizing your desires coming to fruition.
- Enjoy the comforting scent that fills your space, and allow the energy of the simmer pot to enhance your daily life.

Other Elements

Recipes for the Year

January

Carnation

January's New Beginnings Simmer

Ingredients:
2 **Oranges**
2 **Cinnamon Sticks**
Rosemary
Star Anise
Clove

Slice your oranges and add your desired amount of each additional ingredient to your simmer pot. Adjust as needed for preferred aroma.

This aromatic blend embodies the energy of renewal, making it the perfect choice to infuse your space as you embark on a new year. The harmonious dance of ingredients creates a symphony that lingers in the air, ushering in a sense of possibility and excitement.

Notes

_____

_____

_____

_____

_____

Orange Slices (Fresh or Dried): Like sunbursts captured in each slice, oranges bring a burst of vibrant energy. They symbolize the dawn of a new day, their citrusy aroma evoking feelings of warmth and optimism.

Cinnamon Sticks: The rich, comforting scent of cinnamon wafts through the air, reminiscent of freshly baked goods. A symbol of abundance and protection, cinnamon brings a touch of sweetness to the mix, inviting positivity and prosperity.

Rosemary Sprigs: The invigorating aroma of rosemary, like a crisp morning breeze, awakens the senses. Known for its association with remembrance and clarity, rosemary encourages a fresh perspective and sharp focus on new endeavors.

Star Anise: With its elegant, star-shaped form, star anise adds an exotic touch to the blend. Its sweet and licorice-like fragrance fosters a sense of wonder and excitement, reminding us of the mysteries that new beginnings hold.

Cloves: The warm, spicy scent of cloves envelops the senses, grounding the blend with its comforting familiarity. Cloves represent protection and purification, offering a sense of stability as you venture into uncharted territory.

As these ingredients gently simmer, their fragrant dance intertwines, infusing your space with an aroma that evokes the essence of a clean slate. The "January - New Beginnings Simmer" serves as a sensory reminder that each moment offers an opportunity to embrace change, set intentions, and journey into a future rich with possibilities.

February

Violet

February's Love and Connection Simmer

Ingredients:
Rose Petals (dried or fresh)
Vanilla Beans or Extract
Lavender
Cardamom Pods
1 Lemon

Sprinkle your simmer pot with Rose Petals and Lavender. If you don't have access to Vanilla Beans you can substitute with your favorite Vanilla Extract. Adjust the other ingredients as desired.

Invite the essence of love and connection into your space with the "February's Love and Connection Simmer." This aromatic blend encapsulates the warmth of heartfelt emotions, making it an ideal companion as you celebrate relationships and cherish bonds that enrich your life.

Notes

_____

_____

Red Rose Petals: Like delicate confetti, red rose petals infuse the air with their romantic charm. Symbolizing love, passion, and admiration, these petals evoke the timeless sentiment of heartfelt connection.

Vanilla Bean: The sweet and comforting aroma of vanilla envelops the senses, invoking a sense of warmth and familiarity. Vanilla is a symbol of sensuality and comfort, evoking a feeling of closeness and tenderness.

Lavender: Lavender's calming and soothing fragrance wafts through the air, creating an atmosphere of relaxation and inner harmony. Lavender embodies the gentle strength of connection, nurturing bonds that bring peace to the heart.

Cardamom: The exotic and spicy scent of cardamom adds a touch of intrigue to the blend. Known for its associations with love and luck, cardamom pods infuse the air with a sense of enchantment.

Lemon: The invigorating citrus scent of lemon slices adds a zesty and uplifting element to the mix. Lemons symbolize cleansing and freshness, reminding us of the rejuvenating power of authentic connections.

As these ingredients mingle, they create an aromatic that celebrates the depth and beauty of human relationships. Let the fragrant steam be a reminder to nurture the bonds that enrich your life, whether with friends, family, or romantic partners. This simmer pot embodies the essence of connection and love, encouraging you to savor moments of togetherness and celebrate the threads that weave our lives into a fabric of shared experiences.

Spring Equinox

In the realm of nature's dance, a vibrant show,
The Spring Equinox arrives, aglow.
When light and darkness share an equal throne,
A season of rebirth, in nature's zone.

The world awakens from its winter's sleep,
As life from roots to branches starts to creep.
The crocus blooms with hues so bold and bright,
A symphony of colors, pure delight.

As daylight stretches out its warming hand,
The frost retreats, revealing earth's grand plan.
From barren trees, new leaves begin to sprout,
In whispers of the breeze, there's no doubt.

The equinox, a momentary pause,
Between the cold and nature's warming laws.
A balance struck between the day and night,
A fleeting, precious moment, pure and right.

The air is filled with songs of feathered friends,
As winter's chill gives way, and springtime sends
Its blessings forth, with fragrant blooms in tow,
A tapestry of life begins to grow.

The equinox invites us to partake,
In nature's grand awakening, to wake.
To feel the pulse of life in every stream,
And bask in springtime's tender, hopeful gleam.

So, welcome Spring Equinox, with open heart,
As life and light are given a fresh start.
In this season's embrace, we find our way,
In the dance of nature's equinox, we stay.

March

Daffodil

March's
Renewal and Growth Simmer

Ingredients:
Peppermint
Ginger
Thyme
Bay Leaves
Eucalyptus

For this aromatic simmer pot you can use fresh or dried herbs. Freshly sliced Ginger is preferred but dried Ginger is a fine substitute.

Embrace the spirit of renewal and growth with the March Simmer. This aromatic blend encapsulates the energy of nature's awakening, making it an ideal companion as you welcome the transition from winter's slumber to spring's vibrant emergence.

Notes

_____

_____

_____

_____

_____

Peppermint Leaves: The invigorating scent of mint leaves fills the air, evoking a sense of freshness and revitalization. Mint symbolizes rejuvenation and new beginnings, reminding us of the cycle of growth that unfolds each year.

Fresh Ginger Slices: The warm and spicy aroma of fresh ginger slices adds a touch of zest to the blend. Ginger is associated with vitality and energy, reflecting the awakening of nature's forces during the changing seasons.

Thyme Sprigs: Thyme's earthy and aromatic fragrance infuses the air with grounding and stability. Thyme represents strength and courage, serving as a reminder that growth often requires resilience and determination.

Bay Leaves: The rich and herbal scent of bay leaves lends an air of sophistication to the mix. Bay leaves are symbols of achievement and protection, embodying the sense of accomplishment that comes with new growth.

Eucalyptus Leaves: The crisp and invigorating aroma of eucalyptus leaves awakens the senses, reminiscent of fresh air and open spaces. Eucalyptus symbolizes purification and expansion, reflecting the boundless potential of growth and transformation.

In this simmer the elements harmonize and creates an olfactory journey that parallels the unfolding of spring's vitality. Just as nature awakens from its slumber, so too can you embrace the new possibilities that each day brings. This simmer pot captures the essence of spring's promise, encouraging you to bloom and thrive alongside the natural world.

April

Daisy

April's Awakening Simmer

Ingredients:
1 Lemon
Lavender
Jasmine
Rosemary
Spearmint

Slice your lemon and sprinkle in your dry herbs. If needed you can substitute with essential oils. It's always appropriate to use what you have!

Experience the essence of awakening with the April Simmer. This aromatic blend captures the spirit of nature's revival, making it a perfect companion as you embrace the transition from the quietude of winter to the vibrant emergence of spring.

Notes

_____

_____

_____

_____

Lemon Slices: The zesty aroma of lemon slices dances through the air, bringing with it a sense of freshness and vitality. Lemons symbolize cleansing and new beginnings. This gives you the perfect opportunity to mirror the process by shedding the old and welcoming the new.

Lavender Flowers: Lavender's calming fragrance wafts gently, infusing the air with tranquility and serenity. Lavender embodies the balance between awakening and relaxation, reminding us to honor both our energy and our stillness.

Jasmine Flowers: The intoxicating scent of jasmine flowers weaves through the blend, evoking feelings of sensuality and enchantment. Jasmine symbolizes rebirth and renewal, reflecting the transformative power of embracing change.

Rosemary Sprigs: Rosemary's invigorating scent adds a touch of earthiness to the mix, grounding the blend with its aromatic presence. Rosemary represents remembrance and growth, inviting us to honor our past while embracing the journey ahead.

Fresh Mint Leaves: The revitalizing aroma of fresh mint leaves adds a burst of energy to the concoction. Mint signifies clarity and encourages us to approach each day with a refreshed perspective.

As these elements come together in an aromatic symphony that mirrors the natural world's resurgence. Let the fragrant steam serve as a reminder to awaken your senses, embrace the beauty of transformation, and celebrate the blossoming that occurs within and around you. This simmer pot is the embodiment of a new chapter, encouraging you to step into the light of possibility and growth.

May

Lily

May's Abundance and Blossoming Simmer

Ingredients:
Rose Petals, Rose Water, or Rose Essential Oil
Vanilla
2 Cinnamon Sticks
Clove
1 Apple

Slice your apple and add your desired amount of the additional ingredients. Remember that Vanilla Bean is preferred but extract is a perfectly good substitute.

Celebrate the season of abundance and blossoming with the May Simmer Pot recipe. This aromatic blend captures the spirit of nature's generosity, making it an ideal companion as you embrace the richness of life's offerings.

Notes

_____

_____

_____

_____

_____

Rose Petals: The delicate aroma of dried rose petals fills the air, evoking feelings of love and grace. Roses symbolize beauty and abundance, reflecting the lavishness of nature's gifts.

Vanilla Bean or Extract: The warm and comforting scent of vanilla envelops the senses, invoking comfort and indulgence. Vanilla symbolizes richness and pleasure, reminding us to savor life's sweet moments.

Cinnamon Sticks: The inviting scent of cinnamon adds a touch of warmth to the blend. Cinnamon is associated with abundance and prosperity, embodying the idea of reaping the rewards of effort.

Cloves: The spicy and aromatic fragrance of cloves infuses the air with a sense of depth and richness. Cloves represent protection and enhancement, serving as a reminder to cherish and safeguard the blessings that come our way.

Apple Slices: The crisp and fruity scent of apple slices adds a touch of freshness to the mix. Apples symbolize growth and knowledge, reflecting the idea of embracing opportunities and learning from experiences.

As these elements blend they creates an olfactory tapestry that mirrors the lavishness of the natural world's offerings. Allow this fragrant simmer pot to remind you of life's abundance and the blossoming possibilities that each moment holds, it's essence embracing the richness of life, encouraging you to celebrate the myriad blessings that surround you.

June's
Summer Solstice Simmer

Ingredients:
1 Orange
1 Lemon
3 Pineapple Slices
Yarrow
Peppermint

Yarrow can often be found growing on the roadside. It is an easy plant to hang and dry. Add some to your sliced orange and lemon and enjoy the fresh summer aromas.

Celebrate the vibrant energy of the Summer Solstice with the "June - Summer Solstice Celebration Simmer." This aromatic blend captures the essence of sun-soaked days and the joyous spirit of the season's peak.

Notes

_____

_____

_____

_____

_____

Orange Slices: The sun-kissed aroma of orange slices fills the air, evoking a sense of vitality and warmth. Oranges symbolize energy and abundance, reflecting the sun's radiant power.

Lemon Slices: The zesty and invigorating scent of lemon slices adds a touch of freshness to the mix. Lemons symbolize clarity and renewal, reflecting the season's rejuvenating qualities.

Pineapple: The tropical fragrance of pineapple infuses the air with a sense of delight and exoticism. Pineapples symbolize hospitality and friendship, embodying the warmth of summer gatherings.

Yarrow: Yarrow's earthy and herbal fragrance brings a grounding element to the blend. Yarrow represents strength and protection, reminding us to stand firmly in our own light as we celebrate the sun's energy.

Spearmint: The cool and refreshing aroma of spearmint leaves adds a burst of energy to the concoction. Spearmint symbolizes vitality and renewal, encouraging us to fully embrace the season's liveliness.

The June, Summer Solstice Simmer creates an aroma that prompts us to seek the sun's radiant embrace. Let the fragrant steam serve as a reminder to bask in the sun's warmth, embrace the joy of togetherness, and celebrate the vibrant energy of life. This simmer pot epitomizes the heart of the season's peak, encouraging you to revel in the abundant blessings and spirited festivities that define the summer solstice.

July

Larkspur

July's Sunlit Serenity Simmer

Lavender
1 Lemon
Peppermint
Chamomile
Vanilla Beans or Extract

Slice your lemon and add the rest of your ingredients. Remember that substituting extracts or essential oils are just fine and can bring you the same simmer pot enjoyment. In an pinch, you may substitute a lovely Chamomile tea if dried herbs are unavailable.

Indulge in the sunlit serenity that July brings, courtesy of this enchanting simmer. This carefully crafted aromatic blend serves as a gateway to the serene essence of summertime, encapsulating the very tranquility that defines leisurely days under the sun's golden gaze.

Notes

_____

_____

_____

_____

Lavender: The aromatic presence of lavender flowers sweeps through the air, transporting you to fields in full bloom. This sacred herb is renowned for its capacity to promote calm and balance, aligning perfectly with the languid spirit of summertime reflection.

Peppermint Leaves: The invigorating scent of mint leaves fills the air, evoking a sense of vitality and freshness. Mint symbolizes rejuvenation and new beginnings, reminding us of the cycle of growth that unfolds each year.

Lemon Slices: Like drops of sunshine captured within, the slices of lemon radiate their citrusy essence. With each waft, they infuse your surroundings with the vibrancy of clarity, aligning splendidly with the illuminating rays of the season.

Chamomile Flowers: Chamomile's gentle grace envelops the mixture, weaving its delicate presence into the ensemble. A master of tranquility, chamomile bridges the gap between the bustling world and the inner haven of peace, much like the effect of a leisurely day spent outdoors.

Vanilla Bean or Extract: The rich warmth of vanilla cradles the composition, conjuring images of sunsets that cast a golden glow across the horizon. Vanilla, the essence of comfort and nostalgia, wraps the blend in a sense of familiarity that complements the cherished memories cultivated during summer's embrace.

Enriching the ambiance with its allure, the Sunlit Serenity Simmer takes you on a sensory journey through the heart of summer. With each fragrant infusion, it beckons you to pause, breathe, and revel in the harmonious symphony of nature's gifts, inviting you to experience July's sunlit serenity to its fullest extent.

August

Poppy

August
Harvest and Gratitude Simmer

Apple slices
Cinnamon sticks
Nutmeg
Cloves
Bay leaves

Honey Crisp or Jonathan? Either will smell amazing sliced in this simmer pot. Add your cinnamon sticks and dry ingredients to fill your home with the sweet smell of the harvest season.

Celebrate the bountiful spirit of August with the Harvest and Gratitude Simmer." This aromatic blend captures the essence of nature's abundance and encourages a heartwarming sense of gratitude for the gifts of the season.

Notes

_____

_____

_____

_____

_____

Apple Slices: The sweet, crisp scent of apple slices fills the air, reminiscent of orchards heavy with fruit. Apples symbolize the harvest's abundance and the pleasures of sharing the earth's riches.

Cinnamon Sticks: The warming fragrance of cinnamon sticks adds a touch of spice to the blend. Cinnamon embodies the cozy feeling of autumn's approach, representing the comfort of hearth and home.

Nutmeg: The rich and nutty aroma of nutmeg offers depth to the mix. Nutmeg symbolizes transformation and renewal, reflecting the transition from summer's vibrancy to the golden hues of fall.

Cloves: The spicy and aromatic presence of cloves infuses the air with a sense of richness and protection. Cloves represent both preservation and enhancement, echoing the idea of preserving the season's goodness.

Bay Leaves: The herbal and sophisticated scent of bay leaves brings an air of elegance to the blend. Bay leaves symbolize achievement and respect, embodying the recognition of the efforts that lead to a fruitful harvest.

As these ingredients meld together the aroma reflects the richness of nature's offerings during this time of year. Let the fragrant steam serve as a reminder to embrace the blessings of abundance and express gratitude for the many gifts that grace your life. This simmer pot embodies the spirit of a plentiful harvest, encouraging you to savor the flavors and joys of the season while reflecting on the blessings that surround you.

September

Aster

September - Balance and Transition Simmer

Sage leaves (fresh or dried)
Rosemary sprigs
Pine needles
Juniper berries
Thyme sprigs

Take some time to forage for Juniper berries and pine needles. Enjoy the moment with nature and the gifts that it gives. Add all elements to your simmer pot and enjoy.

Find harmony in the transition of September with the "September - Balance and Transition Simmer." This aromatic blend encapsulates the equilibrium of nature's shifts and invites you to embrace the changes that come with the season.

Notes

_____

_____

_____

_____

Sage Leaves (Fresh or Dried): The earthy and grounding aroma of sage leaves graces the air, reminiscent of ancient rituals. Sage represents wisdom and cleansing, symbolizing the importance of clarity during times of change.

Rosemary Sprigs: The invigorating scent of rosemary sprigs adds a touch of energy to the blend. Rosemary embodies resilience and remembrance, encouraging you to stand strong while honoring the past.

Pine Needles: The crisp and outdoorsy fragrance of pine needles infuses the brew with a sense of renewal and growth. Pine symbolizes endurance and purification, mirroring the endurance of life's transitions.

Juniper Berries: The aromatic presence of juniper berries adds a touch of mystique to the ensemble. Juniper is associated with protection and invigoration, reminding you to welcome new experiences with open arms.

Thyme Sprigs: Thyme's fragrant and herbal quality completes the blend, promoting stability and courage. Thyme signifies strength in times of change, encouraging you to navigate transitions with resilience.

As these elements intertwine, allow the Balance and Transition Simmer to create an olfactory experience that reflects the equilibrium of nature's seasonal shifts. Allow the fragrant steam to serve as a reminder to embrace change as a natural part of life's journey, fostering balance and adaptability. This simmer pot embodies the essence of finding stability within transitions, encouraging you to move forward with grace and wisdom during this transformative time of year.

October

Marigold

October
Mystical Energies Simmer

Frankincense Essential oil
Myrrh Essential Oil
2 Cinnamon sticks
Orange slices
Star anise

Conjure up an exquisite simmer pot perfect for the month of October, or any time you are feeling particularly connected to nature's energy. Using essential oils are a convenient way to get the elements you need.

Unveil the mystique of October with the "October - Mystical Energies Simmer." This enchanting blend captures the essence of this mystical month, inviting you to tap into the otherworldly energies that abound.

Notes

_____

_____

_____

_____

_____

Frankincense: The sacred and woody scent of frankincense resin fills the air, invoking a sense of spiritual connection and transcendence. Frankincense has been used for centuries in rituals and meditation to elevate the spirit and enhance focus.

Myrrh: The earthy and resinous aroma of myrrh resin complements the blend, adding depth and grounding. Myrrh is associated with purification and healing, creating a sense of balance and tranquility.

Cinnamon Sticks: The warm and spicy fragrance of cinnamon sticks adds a touch of passion to the mix. Cinnamon symbolizes creativity and vitality, igniting the spark of inspiration and transformation.

Orange Slices: The vibrant citrus scent of orange slices brings a burst of energy to the concoction. Oranges represent joy and abundance, infusing the blend with positivity and enthusiasm.

Star Anise: The exotic and star-shaped presence of star anise adds an air of mystery to the ensemble. Star anise is associated with protection and intuition, enhancing your connection to mystical energies.

As these elements converge, the "October - Mystical Energies Simmer" creates an olfactory tapestry that mirrors the enchanting atmosphere of this unique month. Allow the fragrant steam to serve as a portal to the mystical realms, encouraging you to explore your own spiritual journey and embrace the magic that surrounds you. This simmer pot embodies the essence of October's mysteries, inviting you to tap into your inner wisdom and connect with the mystical energies of the universe.

November

Chrysanthemum

November
Hearth and Home Simmer

Cloves
Vanilla bean or extract
Nutmeg
Cardamom pods
Apple slices

Slice your favorite apple and add a few drops of Vanilla
Extract or whole Vanilla Bean. Incorporate your dry
elements and enjoy. Dry Cardamon can be used in place of
Cardamom pods as needed.

Enjoy the cozy warmth that can be brought by the delicious smells of the November - Hearth and Home Simmer. This blend of spices and extracts simply encapsulates the essence of hearth and home, inviting you to savor the comforts of the season. This is the perfect simmer to put on when expecting the company of friends and family.

Notes

_____

_____

_____

Cloves: The spicy and aromatic presence of cloves infuses the air, reminiscent of a home filled with freshly baked goods. Cloves symbolize protection and comfort, creating a sense of security and nostalgia.

Vanilla Bean or Extract: The rich and comforting scent of vanilla envelops the senses, invoking a sense of coziness and familiarity. Vanilla represents warmth and togetherness, echoing the bonds formed within the heart of the home.

Nutmeg: The warm and nutty aroma of nutmeg offers depth and richness to the mix. Nutmeg symbolizes abundance and tradition, reflecting the age-old customs that make each home unique.

Cardamom Pods: The exotic and spicy fragrance of cardamom pods adds a touch of intrigue to the ensemble. Cardamom is associated with love and unity, reminding you of the love and unity fostered within the home.

Apple Slices: The sweet and crisp scent of apple slices infuses the blend with a touch of freshness. Apples symbolize gratitude and family, embodying the importance of gathering around the hearth with loved ones.

As these elements come together, the Hearth and Home Simmer brings a sense of nostalgia and remembrance to this season. Allow the fragrant steam to serve as a reminder to appreciate the joys of hearth and home, celebrating the traditions and connections that make your space uniquely yours. This simmer pot embodies the essence of November's coziness, encouraging you to find solace and happiness in the heart of your home.

Winter Solstice

In the depths of winter, when daylight wanes,
A celestial dance in the heavens reigns.
The world is hushed in the solstice's embrace,
As the sun's low arc paints a tranquil space.

On the shortest day, the longest night's descent,
A cosmic ballet of time well-spent.
The Earth tilts back, its axis keenly traced,
In this celestial waltz, so perfectly spaced.

The sun, a feeble ember in the sky,
Casts long, enchanting shadows, far and nigh.
Yet in the darkness, a promise is unfurled,
For from this point, the days reclaim the world.

Beneath the starry canopy's display,
A quiet magic fills the air this day.
As nature slumbers, wrapped in winter's cloak,
The solstice whispers secrets that invoke.

We gather 'round the fire's warming glow,
To honor nature's rhythms as they flow.
In this sacred moment, we find our grace,
Celebrating winter's solstice's embrace.

With candles, evergreens, and hearts aglow,
We mark the turning of the wheel, we know.
The return of light, a hopeful, shining glance,
In the heart of winter's solstice, we dance.

So on this night, in quiet reverence here,
We welcome back the sun, without a fear.
For though the world in darkness may be held,
The winter solstice's promise is upheld.

As daylight's strength begins to reemerge,
In nature's grand design, we find our urge.
To cherish every moment, come what may,
In the winter solstice's soft, golden ray.

December

Narcissus

December
Winter Solstice
Reflection Simmer

Pine needles
Juniper berries
Rosemary sprigs
Bay leaves
2 Cinnamon sticks

Add two sticks of Cinnamon and your foraged Pine Needles to your simmering water. The additional elements will add a perfect spicy sweetness to your pot! Enjoy!

The introspective spirit of December is alive in the Winter Solstice Reflection Simmer." It perfectly captures the essence of the winter solstice, inviting you to pause, reflect, and find solace in the quiet beauty of the season.

Notes

_____

_____

_____

_____

Pine Needles: The crisp and outdoorsy fragrance of pine needles infuses the air, reminiscent of a tranquil forest under a blanket of snow. Pine symbolizes endurance and purification, encouraging you to find strength in stillness.

Juniper Berries: The aromatic presence of juniper berries adds a touch of mystique to the ensemble. Juniper is associated with protection and renewal, reminding you of the boundless potential that accompanies the turning of the seasons.

Rosemary Sprigs: The invigorating scent of rosemary sprigs adds a touch of energy to the blend. Rosemary embodies remembrance and growth, inspiring you to honor the past while looking toward the future.

Bay Leaves: The herbal and sophisticated scent of bay leaves brings an air of elegance to the blend. Bay leaves represent achievement and respect, encouraging you to celebrate your accomplishments and honor your path.

Cinnamon Sticks: The warming fragrance of cinnamon sticks adds a touch of coziness to the mix. Cinnamon symbolizes comfort and tradition, inviting you to find warmth in the familiarity of the season.

Together these elements creates an aromatic union that truly represents the serene atmosphere of the winter solstice. Allow this time to serve as a reminder to pause and embrace the quiet beauty of this season, finding solace in reflection and gratitude for the journey that has brought you to this moment. As the year comes to and end this simmer pot embodies the essence of December's introspection, encouraging you to connect with your inner wisdom and find peace in the stillness of winter's embrace.

More Recipes

Additional Simmer Pot Recipes

Here's your opportunity to embark on a culinary experiment! The simmer pot recipes provided include ingredients without specific quantities. Why? Because this is your chance to become intimately acquainted with these components and determine your preferred usage. Perhaps, for me, five cinnamon sticks hit the sweet spot, but for you, it might seem excessive. These ingredient lists serve as mere suggestions, leaving the quantity decision up to you. Don't forget to document your findings! If a particular aroma captivates your senses, make sure to jot it down. Conversely, if a scent doesn't quite align with your preferences, make a note of that too. Towards the end of this section, you'll find a space to create your own simmer pot concoctions. Discover what suits your taste and feel free to share your discoveries with others!

Sleepy Time Simmer

Lavender
Anise
Nutmeg
Cinnamon Sticks
Cloves

Harvest Moon Simmer

Orange Peel or Slices
Bay Leaves
Cinnamon Sticks
Lemon Slices
Allspice

Autumn Apples Simmer

Sliced Apple
Vanilla Bean or Extract
Cloves
Cinnamon Sticks

Notes:

_____

_____

_____

Seasons Greetings Simmer

Clove
Cranberries
Cinnamon Sticks
Orange Slices
Apple Slices
Lemon Slices
Nutmeg
Anise

Chai and Spices Simmer

Cardamom
Cinnamon Sticks
Cloves
Ginger Slices or Dried

Winter Delight Simmer

Rosemary Sprigs
Rose Water or Petals
Cinnamon Sticks
Orange Peel or Slices

Notes:

_____

_____

_____

Summer Sensation Simmer

Vanilla Bean or Extract
Sliced Orange
Sliced Lemon

Wake Up Simmer

Coffee Grounds or Whole Beans
Vanilla Beans or Extract
Cinnamon Sticks

Gingerbread Visions Simmer

Cinnamon Sticks
Nutmeg
Cloves
Cardamom
Anise
Ginger
Allspice

Notes:
_____

_____

_____

_____

_____

Get Mellow Simmer

Lime slices
Spearmint or Peppermint
Thyme
Vanilla Bean or Extract

Holiday Hygge Simmer

Orange Slices or Peel
Cedar Sprigs
Bay Leaves
Rosemary

Forest Feels Simmer

Eucalyptus Sprig or Oil
Sandalwood
Pine
Patchouli

Notes:
_____
_____
_____
_____

Citrus Spice Delight Simmer
Lemon Slices
Spearmint or Peppermint
Thyme
Cinnamon Sticks

Sunny New Beginnings Simmer
Ginger
Oranges
Bay Leaves
Cloves

Winter Bonfire Simmer
Coffee Beans or Grounds
Cedar Springs
Rosemary Springs
Balsam
Basil

Notes:
_____

_____

_____

_____

Woodsy Wonder Simmer

Orange Slices or Peel
Juniper Berrics
Juniper Sprigs
Rosemary

Summer Spice Simmer

Sage
Thyme
Lemon
Grapefruit
Lavender
Ginger

Floral Fantasy Simmer

Rose Water or Petals
Lavender
Black Tea
Chamomile
Lemon Slices or Peel

Notes:

_____

_____

_____

_____

Sooth Your Soul Simmer

Lavender Essential Oil or Dried Springs
Eucalyptus Essential Oil
Rosemary
Sliced Lemon

Sunshine Simmer

Lime Slices or Peel
Ginger
Spearmint
Thyme
Eucalyptus

Fireside Simmer

Cinnamon Sticks
Peppermint
Cardamom
Black Tea

Notes:
_____
_____
_____
_____
_____
_____

Full Moon Simmer
Sage
Sandalwood
Patchouli
Vanilla

New Year Simmer
Grapefruit Slices or Peel
Basil
Lavender

Rainy Day Simmer
Vanilla
Black Tea
Lavender
Black Pepper

_____

_____

_____

_____

_____

My Recipes

Acknowledgements

S. Theresa Dietz, The Complete Language of Herbs, A Definitive & Illustrated History, (Quarto Publishing Group 2022)

S. Theresa Dietz, The Complete Language of Flowers, A Definitive and Illustrated History, (Quarto Publishing Group 2020)

Gathering Dreams, www.gatheringdreams.com

The Outdoor Apothecary, www.outdoorapothercary.com

Apartment Therapy, www.apartmenttherapy.com

I Am A Food Blog, www.Iamafoodblog.com

Home Made Lovely, www.homemadelovely.com

Images provided through Canva.com

The Valkyrie Mystic, www.thevalkyriemystic.com

Wikipedia, www.wikipedia.org

Made in the USA
Las Vegas, NV
20 December 2024

14949839R00075